HIGH-TECH CAREERS

Careers in Robotics

Kathryn Hulick

For more information, contact:
ReferencePoint Press, Inc.
PO Box 27779
San Diego, CA 92198
www.ReferencePointPress.com

LIBRARY OF CONGRESS CATALOGING-IN-PUBLICATION DATA

Names: Hulick, Kathryn, author.
Title: Careers in Robotics / By Kathryn Hulick.
Description: San Diego, CA : ReferencePoint Press, Inc., 2017. | Series: High-tech careers | Includes bibliographical references and index.
Identifiers: LCCN 2016040554 (print) | LCCN 2016040814 (ebook) | ISBN 9781682821183 (hardback) | ISBN 9781682821190 (eBook)
Subjects: LCSH: Robotics--Vocational guidance--Juvenile literature. | Robotics--Juvenile literature.
Classification: LCC TJ211.25 .G37 2017 (print) | LCC TJ211.25 (ebook) | DDC 629.8/92023--dc23
LC record available at https://lccn.loc.gov/2016040554

Contents

Introduction

Robots Are the Future

Robots are everywhere. They put cars together on factory assembly lines. They assist with medical procedures. They vacuum people's floors. In the military, robots defuse and dispose of bombs while drones spy on enemies. On Mars a robot explores the planet's surface and sends pictures and data back to Earth. Other robots explore the deep sea and outer space. In general, robots go places and do things that are too dangerous, dirty, difficult, boring, or repetitive for humans. But they are starting to take over other tasks as well. Robotics technology is what allows a self-driving car to navigate without a person at the wheel. Robots are also starting to educate children and care for the elderly.

In an article for *Forbes*, reporter Alex Knapp placed robotics second on a list of the top majors that college students should consider. "The advent of personal service robots means that the elderly can live longer on their own before going to retirement homes," writes Knapp. "Many other industries are turning to robots as well, including the fast-growing health care industry. This will create a huge need for people in the robotics industry, from programming to engineering."

An Interdisciplinary Field

Any person who works on robots may be called a roboticist. The role of roboticist brings together many other disciplines, including mechanical engineering and computer science. While many people working in the robotics industry today specialize in just one of these fields, a more interdisciplinary education in robotics engineering is becoming more common. Chris Jones is the director for research advancement at iRobot, a company that makes cleaning robots. In an interview on

KidsAhead.com, he said: "Robotics will be always be fairly unique in that it brings together many disciplines—electrical engineering, mechanical engineering, system engineering, computer science and even psychology gets pulled in to help figure how robots can interact with people around them."

In other words a roboticist must have a wide and varied skill set. Brett Kennedy, a roboticist at NASA's Jet Propulsion Laboratory, agrees. In an interview on NASA's website, he said: "Of all the engineering fields, robotics requires the widest understanding and application of topics. Therefore, you're always learning and doing different things."

Hands-on experience is perhaps the single most important way for students interested in robotics to get a head start toward a career in this exciting industry. Organizations such as FIRST Robotics offer opportunities for high school students and younger children to build robots and test them in competitions. Through these learning opportunities, students get a chance to see firsthand how the robot's mechanical, electrical, and computer systems work together. They also must engage in creative problem solving as a team. In addition, robotics engineers, research scientists, technicians, and other roboticists often coach these teams. Students who participate get a chance to meet mentors who are already working in the robotics industry.

A Surging Market

The robotics industry is divided into two markets: industrial robots and service robots. Some industrial robots take the form of robotic arms, welders, and machining tools that put products together on assembly lines. Others carry material or products from place to place in a factory, warehouse, or distribution center. Service robots include robots intended for home use, medical purposes, the military, and self-driving vehicles. A 2015 report from the research firm Tractica predicts that the robotics market will more than quadruple in value between 2015 and 2020, from $28.3 billion to $151.7 billion. The report predicts that nonindustrial robots will account for most of this growth. "Around the world, new players and markets are emerging to assume an important role in the ongoing development of the robotics industry," Tractica research director Aditya Kaul said in the report.

Careers in Robotics

Occupation	Entry-Level Education	2015 Median Pay
Computer and Information Research Scientist	Doctoral or professional degree	$110,620
Computer Hardware Engineer	Bachelor's degree	$111,730
Computer Programmer	Bachelor's degree	$79,530
Electrical and Electronics Engineer	Bachelor's degree	$95,230
Electrical and Electronics Engineering Technician	Associate's degree	$61,130
Machinist and Tool and Die Maker	High school diploma or equivalent	$42,110
Mechanical Engineering Technician	Associate's degree	$53,910
Metal and Plastic Machine Worker	High school diploma or equivalent	$34,080
Sales Engineer	Bachelor's degree	$97,650
Software Engineer	Bachelor's degree	$100,690

Source: Bureau of Labor Statistics, *Occupational Outlook Handbook*. www.bls.gov/ooh.

"Technologies like AI, machine vision, voice and speech recognition, tactile sensors, and gesture control will drive robotic capabilities far beyond what is possible today, especially in terms of autonomy."

Companies are looking to hire engineers, technicians, programmers, and others who can develop robots with all of these advanced capabilities. But people with the right skill set are hard to find. In an article for *Fortune* magazine, reporter Anne Fisher wrote: "The shortage of people who know how to build, program, maintain, and repair robots has gotten so severe that, in some parts of the country, qualified candidates can practically write their own ticket."

As a result, salaries are high for robotics engineers. They earn a median wage of $81,267 and have the potential to earn over six figures. Professionals with a background in computer science and programming can expect to find the most job opportunities and earn the highest salaries in the robotics industry. Jones supports this analysis. He said: "There is a very emerging market for robotics, as well as a very rich academic research environment. One area that will probably grow the most or show the most impact is computer science. We are going to start seeing more sophistication and increased capabilities being put into robots through the addition of intelligent software."

Will a Robot Steal Your Job?

Whenever a new kind of robot rises in importance, people start to worry about losing their jobs to machines. For example, right now, self-driving vehicles threaten the livelihoods of truck drivers and taxi drivers. Though these are very real concerns, the lost jobs are typically replaced with new, different jobs. Those self-driving vehicles will need people who can build, program, and maintain them. Matt Zeigler works for Motoman, an industrial robotics company in Ohio. In his opinion the rise of the robots is a good thing. "It's actually creating better jobs and better-paying jobs," he said in an interview with CNN. "They're just more technical and not as repetitive."

Ty Tremblay, a field systems engineer at a robotics company, comments that at least one job is safe. In an interview with the author, he said, "If you're building robots, you will never have your industry disappear in your lifetime."

Robotics Engineer

What Does a Robotics Engineer Do?

Robotics engineers design, maintain, and test robots. The majority of robotics engineers work with industrial robots, such as the ones that put cars together on an assembly line or the ones that sort pallets at a distribution center. Others work on the cutting edge of robotics technology, designing robots to explore outer space or the deep sea, developing robots for disaster response, or using them for medical or military purposes.

At a Glance: Robotics Engineer

Minimum Educational Requirements
Bachelor's degree

Personal Qualities
Creativity; attention to detail; problem-solving skills; affinity for science, math, and computer programming

Working Conditions
Mostly indoors

Salary Range
About $52,667 to $105,816

Number of Jobs
As of 2014 about 137,000 in the United States

Future Job Outlook
Expected increase of 4 percent through 2022

Robotics engineering is an emerging field that combines aspects of mechanical, electrical, and software engineering. The best robotics engineers are skilled in all of these areas, but many specialize in one of the three. Mechanical engineering corresponds to the robot's body. A robotics engineer with a mechanical background might investigate materials for building a robot or develop its structure. Electrical engineering helps bring the robot to life. A robotics engineer who focuses on this area might develop sensor systems to allow the robot to detect its environment, electrical systems to move it around, or control systems so people can operate the robot. Finally, software engineering gives the robot a brain. A robotics engineer who works on software writes programs to allow a robot to interact with the world and take specific actions.

iRobot, a company famous for its vacuum-cleaning Roomba line of robots, has a whole team of robotics engineers. "They do a lot of the innovating, and get tasked with a lot of really challenging problems," Corey Russell, an employee of iRobot, explained in an interview with the author. However, the job title of robotics engineer remains uncommon in the workplace today. Though many companies are looking to hire people with degrees or experience in robotics engineering, their roles are typically more specialized. Russell's title is Test Engineer, even though he has a degree in robotics engineering. As a test engineer, he works with robots every day, but instead of designing them, he makes sure that they work the way they are supposed to.

Ty Tremblay has his master's degree in robotics engineering, but his official title is Field Systems Engineer at a robotics company. A systems engineer focuses on designing a complex system so that all of its components work together smoothly. This often includes troubleshooting problems and modifying the system to increase efficiency. In Tremblay's case the system happens to be a group of more than a hundred robots driving around a warehouse to pick up items needed to fulfill customer orders.

People with robotics engineering degrees may also work as industrial engineers or control engineers. An industrial engineer is similar to a systems engineer but typically focuses more on the practical application of the system rather than its design. Controls engineering utilizes mathematical modeling to develop controls for a system so that it will perform in the desired way.

Rich Hooper is a robotics engineer at a company that designs and builds custom robots. He describes his typical day on his website, Learn About Robots:

> I spend two or three hours designing electrical circuits or mechanical systems and helping younger engineers learn about these circuits and systems and an hour or two working on Bills of Materials (BOM's). This is a list of all the materials in the system. It includes wires,

resistors, integrated circuits, nuts, bolts and processors, etc. The manufacturing department uses the BOM's and the drawings to build the systems. [Then I spend] an hour or two in meetings or conference calls, an hour or two writing emails, and an hour or two in the lab conducting experiments or trying to understand why the systems I designed are not working the way I thought they would. . . . I usually sneak in a few hours working early in the morning on weekends. I typically work 53-hour weeks.

How Do You Become a Robotics Engineer?

Education

A bachelor's degree in robotics engineering opens up opportunities in many different industries and engineering fields. Robotics engineering degree programs are growing in popularity at colleges and universities. Though the specific courses required differ from school to school, every program will include classes in mechanical, electrical, and software engineering, as well as some classes in robotics. A robotics class may cover control systems or programmable logic systems for directing robots, computer-aided design or manufacturing for designing robots, or the principles of hydraulics and pneumatics to make the robot move.

Some people who complete a bachelor's program in this interdisciplinary field go on to get a master's degree or PhD. While this level of education is not required for most robotics engineering positions, it may be necessary to work in artificial intelligence or other cutting-edge areas.

Compared with other engineering majors, robotics engineering "definitely takes more effort, more time, and a dedicated person to complete the program," Joseph St. Germain said in an interview with the author. He manages the robotics lab at Worcester Polytechnic Institute.

In addition to a college education, robotics engineers also need hands-on experience designing and building robots. Many people working in this field today got their start participating in robotics competitions or just tinkering in their spare time. Fernando Zumbado, a robotics systems engineer at NASA, describes on NASA.gov how his robotics education began:

> When I was an undergraduate student at Northwestern University, I stumbled into the yearly robotics competition held every spring. I was planning only to check out what all the people were watching, but I ended up staying for the whole event—all four hours! I was consumed by all the different solutions the teams had conjured for the maze they needed to navigate. Shortly after, I enrolled in robotics courses in the engineering school and chose robotics as the concentration for my mechanical engineering degree. I also applied to work at NASA's Johnson Space Center in Houston. . . . Once hired at Johnson, I began working in the robotics group and enjoyed the cutting-edge technology work.

Students do not have to wait until college to take part in robotics competitions. These competitions are offered internationally for K–12 students through organizations such as FIRST. In the FIRST Robotics Competition, teams of high school students get six weeks to build a robot that will have to play a game against other teams' robots. The competition challenges participants to solve problems that involve science, technology, engineering, and math. FIRST LEGO League offers similar competitions for elementary and middle school students.

Internships

Many robotics engineering students seek out summer internships while still in college. NASA offers a Robotics Academy program. This ten-week internship assigns participants to work on a project with NASA, a local industry, or an academic institution. "It's a very hot field right now, so there are a lot of internship opportunities," says St. Germain.

Skills and Personality

Robotics engineers must be problem solvers who enjoy math, science, technology, and figuring out how things work. They may spend their spare time taking apart machines and putting them back together again. Creativity helps these engineers come up with innovative solutions, while attention to detail keeps them focused on the task at hand. Eugene Kozlenko is a mechanical engineer who works on robotic limbs. In an article on the website WetFeet, he explains that he is constantly coming up with creative solutions to problems: "You can't go more than a few hours without having to come up with something clever. Whether it's the most cost-effective way to machine a particular part, or coming up with a way to test a circuit that narrows down which component is acting up—every day is full of little opportunities."

In addition to problem-solving skills, communication is also important, as almost all robotics engineers collaborate with others on a team. Finally, robotics engineers must be passionate about their work. Corey Russell says, "You have to have a lot of drive. You have to really care about what you're doing, because every so often you're going to have to pull several 16-hour days in a row to get stuff done in time."

Employers

Industrial robots are the most common kind of robot used in the world today, with 221,000 units sold in 2014. Consequently, the majority of robotics engineering jobs involve designing, improving, and troubleshooting industrial robots. Industrial robotics companies include ABB Robotics, which supplies robots for manufacturing tasks, and Aethon, which develops mobile robots for transporting, delivering, and tracking materials.

All other commercially sold robots are called service robots; 24,207 of these devices were sold in 2014. Companies such as General Dynamics and Lockheed Martin hire robotics engineers to produce service robots for the military. Google needs robotics engineers to work on its self-driving cars. At NASA, robotics engineers build robots to explore other planets.

Working Conditions

Robotics engineers typically work indoors in an office, lab, or factory. They usually work with teams of engineers and other specialists, each with a unique skill set. They often put in more than forty hours every week. Some engineers may have to travel to install or inspect robots at remote locations.

Earnings

A robotics engineer in an entry-level position earns about $52,667 per year as of 2016, according to the website PayScale.com. A senior engineer could earn as much as $105,816. As of 2015, the median income for all robotics engineers is $81,267. That's just slightly better than average for all engineering careers, but double the median income for all Americans. An engineer in the robotics industry who develops software will typically earn more than someone who concentrates on electrical or mechanical engineering.

Opportunities for Advancement

Robotics engineers typically enter the industry as an associate-level engineer. From there, they may advance to a particular specialty, such as test engineer, controls engineer, or robotics engineer. After being in that position for a number of years, they may be promoted to senior engineers. Robotics engineers with good communication and interpersonal skills may become managers. In this role the engineer leads a team of people to design, improve, or maintain robots and robotic systems. Because robotics engineers develop a range of skills across different fields of engineering, they are typically able to move to new roles or new industries more easily than other engineers.

What Is the Future Outlook for Robotics Engineers?

The field of robotics is growing thanks to major advances in robotic technology. As this field continues to expand, robotic engineers will be in demand. Although the Bureau of Labor Statistics predicts just 4 percent growth for this particular job through 2022, the market for robots is expected to grow quite a lot. A report from Markets and Markets says that the industrial robot market should grow 12 percent between 2016 and 2022, and a separate report from Zion Market Research predicts a whopping 18 percent growth in sales of service robots between 2015 and 2020. The robotics industry will be hiring many different kinds of engineers to support this growth. Yi Lu Murphey, chair of the Department of Electrical and Computer Engineering at the University of Michigan, was quoted in the blog *Product Lifecycle Report*: "The field of robotics engineering is booming. It promises to be the next growing frontier for engineers."

Find Out More

International Federation of Robotics (IFR)
Lyoner Str. 18, 60528 Frankfurt am Main
Germany
website: www.ifr.org

The IFR seeks to promote and strengthen the robotics industry worldwide, as well as to increase public awareness of robotics technologies.

Robotics & Automation Society (RAS)
445 Hoes Ln.
Piscataway Township, NJ 08854
website: www.ieee-ras.org

The RAS is a group within the Institute of Electrical and Electronics Engineers that promotes the exchange of scientific and technical knowledge in robots and automation. Through journals, newsletters, and meetings, the group spreads news, facilitates research, and documents best practices in the industry.

Robotics Industries Association (RIA)
900 Victors Way
Ann Arbor, MI 48106
website: www.robotics.org

The RIA is a trade association that serves the industrial robotics industry. It offers training seminars and tutorials to address safety issues and risk assessment. Its goals include education, innovation, growth, and safety in the industry. Members range from robot manufacturers and robot users to research groups.

Society of Manufacturing Engineers (SME)

1 SME Dr.
Dearborn, MI 48128
website: www.sme.org/ama

The SME serves the manufacturing community. Its goals include promoting new technology and developing a skilled workforce. The Automated Manufacturing & Assembly Community is a group within the SME that focuses on robots and automation in manufacturing.

FIRST

200 Bedford St.
Manchester, NH 03101
website: www.firstinspires.org

This organization sponsors the FIRST Robotics Competition, involving student-built robots competing against each other. The competition challenges participants to solve problems that involve science, technology, engineering, and math. FIRST LEGO League offers similar competitions for elementary and middle school students.

Robotics Technician

What Does a Robotics Technician Do?

At a Glance: Robotics Technician

Minimum Educational Requirements
Associate's degree or technical certificate

Personal Qualities
Attention to detail; dexterity and ease working with tools; enjoys problem solving, logic, and math

Certification and Licensing
Voluntary

Working Conditions
Varied; typically either a sterile laboratory or factory production floor

Salary Range
About $31,912 to $71,184*

Number of Jobs
As of 2014 about 14,700 in the United States*

Future Job Outlook
1 percent through 2024*

*Numbers are for electromechanical technicians, a group that includes robotics technicians.

Robotics technicians build, test, install, operate, maintain, and repair robots. They have to understand how machines, electronics, and computers work. This hands-on job involves the use of precision instruments and tools to put robots together and take them apart. These technicians also program or repair the computer systems that run robots.

A robotics technician typically works under an engineer. While the engineer is responsible for the overall design and function of the robot, the technician is usually the one physically handling the robot. Most robotics technicians fall into one of two categories: The first type is a technician who works on robots during the product development process, before they are sold to customers. The second is a technician who works with robots on the job, typically in industrial manufacturing.

Technicians involved in the robot design process work directly with engineers at a robotics company. In this role a technician may order parts, build the physical structure of a robot, develop its electrical systems, or assist with writing computer programs to control the robot. A technician also helps test new robots and troubleshoot errors. Corey Russell is a robotics engineer at iRobot who tests robots to make sure that they function properly. In an interview with the author, he explained the role of a technician who works for him. "[He is] the one actually running the tests—running around, starting robots here and there, recording what happens, and collecting data from the robot when it finishes."

Technicians who work with robots once they've been put to work at a factory may specialize in one of several roles. Robotics trainers typically work for a robot manufacturer. They travel to factories that purchased a robot or robot system to help train employees there to operate and maintain it. Robotics maintenance technicians, on the

Some robotics technicians are troubleshooters. When problems arise, especially on the factory floor, technicians search for the cause in an effort to restore proper function to robotics equipment and keep the process moving.

other hand, are typically employed by the factory. They troubleshoot any errors that occur, and perform regular maintenance to ensure that robots and their computer systems work properly. Their goal is to reduce downtime in order to keep the factory's assembly line churning along. Jessica Amsden is a robotics technician who works in a factory. In a video from the National Institute for Women in Trades, Technology and Science, she said:

> When there's a breakdown, I will discuss with the operator what the problem is. [Then] I will go in and adjust sensors, or find mechanical defects. Springs can become weak. Moving parts can eventually hit each other. Errors or glitches [can occur] in the program which runs the actual assembly line. It could be any of these. . . . One of the most important skills is troubleshooting. You really have to be able to look at a machine and track down the problem from start to finish.

How Do You Become a Robotics Technician?

Education

Robotics technicians and engineers often work together and perform similar tasks. The main difference between these two roles is the amount of education required. While an engineer must complete a four-year bachelor's degree program, a technician only requires an associate's degree or postsecondary certificate from a two-year program at a community college, vocational school, or technical school. Some technicians may get hired with only a high school diploma, as long as they have mechanical skills as well as a strong background in math and science.

The degree or certificate program to become a robotics technician may focus on one of several fields, including electromechanics, industrial maintenance, and mechatronics. Mechatronics is a field that combines aspects of mechanical engineering, electrical engineering, control systems, and computer programming. In these programs students learn about programmable logic controllers, sensors, electronics, computer-aided design software, and a variety of approaches for the control and automation of machines and mechanical processes. David Adams is an instructor at Utah Valley University. In a video on the school's website, he describes their degree program in Electrical Automation and Robotics Technology:

> In the first semester we teach the basic electrical math and theory . . . it's the foundation of our entire program. . . . In the second semester . . . we get into lots of different controls for AC motors and DC motors . . . and we teach the students how to design circuits that are functional . . . we also teach them troubleshooting.

Certification and Licensing

Certification is not required to work as a robotics technician. However, some technicians choose to obtain certification in order to demonstrate their competence or to work with a particular type of technology. A variety of different certifications are available from professional organizations and educational institutions. The International Society of Automation offers a Certified Control Systems Technician program. There are three different levels of certification, based on the number of years of work experience and the amount of education the candidate has. In addition to this experience, a candidate must take an exam in order to qualify.

Volunteer Work and Internships

Technical degree programs in robotics or automation typically encourage students to participate in internships or apprenticeship programs that combine on-the-job experience and training with course work. Completing a paid internship may be a required component of the program.

Students in these degree programs often volunteer as coaches or mentors to high school robotics teams. They may also participate in robotics competitions themselves to hone their skills. For example, robotics students at Dunwoody College of Technology in Minnesota regularly participate in the Institute of Navigation autonomous snowplow competition. Instructor E.J. Daigle said in a 2016 press release about the contest that the best part was his team's "cooperative competition." This type of activity helps prepare students for the workforce, where they must also cooperate to solve problems with limited time and materials.

Skills and Personality

First and foremost, a robotics technician must enjoy the hands-on work of building, installing, and repairing machinery and electronics. Successful technicians know how things work, and like taking things apart and putting them back together. They have excellent hand-eye coordination, manual dexterity, and spatial sense. Alex Jensen started out studying electrical engineering. He explains why he switched to a technician program in a video on Utah Valley University's website: "I wanted something a little more hands on, a little more in the field working in electronics." Another student at the same school, Jeremy Giles, added, "It's a good vocational choice for anyone who wants to learn how to make things go. . . . It's a good choice for women, men, anyone interested in that."

While technicians spend more time working directly with robots, they have a lot of skills in common with robotics engineers. They also must be adept problem solvers who pay close attention to detail. Communication is also an important skill, as technicians must work closely with engineers, robot operators, and others. In addition, technicians need to read, write, and understand technical documentation and reports.

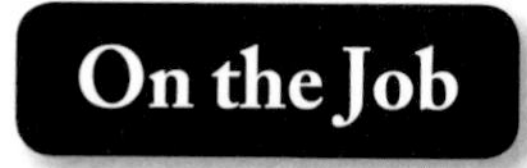

Employers

Manufacturers that use robots on their assembly lines hire the most robotics technicians. Examples include automotive manufacturers, such as General Motors; 3M, a company that makes office products; and Bühler, a manufacturer of flour, pasta, chocolate, and other foodstuffs.

Robotics technicians work in many other industries as well. They can typically be found at any employer that hires robotics engineers, such as iRobot, which designs cleaning robots, or Boston Dynamics, which designs robots for military use. Robotics technicians also work for the Defense Department of the US government to design, build, test, and maintain robots that detect and defuse bombs. In the medical industry, technicians install or repair robots used in operations and other procedures.

Working Conditions

Robotics technicians on the design side of the industry usually work in a laboratory environment, though they may also work outdoors to test larger robots or self-driving vehicles. A robotics lab may be a sterile environment that requires protective clothing, caps, and gloves to enter. These precautions protect sensitive equipment from stray dirt, hair, or sweat. Sterile labs can also be found at some manufacturing plants, such as the one where Jessica Amsden works. She performs most of her repairs in the dry room. "[It] is a very sensitive area," she says. "So before I go into the dry room, I have to get dressed in protective clothing."

Technicians employed in factories may also work out on the production floor. This is often a noisy, busy environment. Robotics technicians typically stay on their feet all day long and work a forty-hour week. Robotics technicians in manufacturing may need to come in on nights or weekends if sensitive equipment breaks, or may have maintenance work scheduled over holiday periods. Travel is required for some robotics technicians, especially those who assist customers with robot installation, training, or repairs.

Earnings

Robotics technicians typically earn an hourly wage. According to the Bureau of Labor Statistics (BLS), this can range from $13.30 up to $27.20 per hour. The rate depends on the technician's education and experience, as well as the location of the job. The annual wages for a technician range from about $31,912 to $71,184. As of 2015 the median wage for all American workers was $36,200. So a technician can expect to earn right around that median wage at his or her first job. A technician skilled in programming will typically earn more than one with an electrical or mechanical background. In addition, if a technician is able and willing to work overtime, his or her compensation will greatly increase.

Opportunities for Advancement

Robotics technicians do not typically receive substantial raises as they increase their skills and experience. However, they usually have the opportunity to move on to new roles within the same company. Some technicians complete bachelor's degree programs while working and advance to engineering positions. Others move up to work in sales, or as a manager.

What Is the Future Outlook for Robotics Technicians?

While demand still exists for robotics technicians in the United States, the field is growing very slowly. The BLS predicts just 1 percent growth through 2024. The reason for this slow growth is that many manufacturing companies in the United States are shutting down or moving overseas. In addition, robotic machinery is becoming increasingly efficient, requiring less care and maintenance. Better robots mean that factories require fewer human employees. However, technicians and engineers are still needed to design and build those robots.

Technicians work in many areas other than manufacturing. The market for service robots for homes and offices is predicted to grow 18 percent between 2015 and 2020, according to a 2016 report from Zion Market Research. The demand for military robots and medical robots is also growing. All of these industries will need technicians to work alongside engineers.

Motion Control & Motor Association
900 Victors Way, Suite 140
Ann Arbor, MI 48108
website: www.motioncontrolonline.org

This trade association seeks to advance understanding of motion control and automation technology, and to promote growth in these industries. It provides support and leadership on common industry issues. It also performs market research, organizes a forum and trade show, and runs educational workshops and conferences.

Robotics & Automation Society (RAS)

445 Hoes Ln.
Piscataway Township, NJ 08854
website: www.ieee-ras.org

The RAS is a group within the Institute of Electrical and Electronics Engineers that promotes the exchange of scientific and technical knowledge in robots and automation. Through journals, newsletters, and meetings, the group spreads news, facilitates research, and documents best practices in the industry.

Robotics Industries Association (RIA)

900 Victors Way
Ann Arbor, MI 48106
website: www.robotics.org

The RIA is a trade association that serves the industrial robotics industry. It offers training seminars and tutorials to address safety issues and risk assessment. Its goals include education, innovation, growth, and safety in the industry. Members range from robot manufacturers and robot users to research groups.

Technology Student Association (TSA)

1914 Association Dr.
Reston, VA 20191
website: www.tsaweb.org

This national organization is open to students enrolled in science, technology, engineering, and math courses. The organization offers leadership and learning opportunities for students through competitive events, conferences, and service projects. The TSA's membership includes more than 233,000 middle and high school students in approximately two thousand schools spanning forty-nine states.

FIRST

200 Bedford St.
Manchester, NH 03101
website: www.firstinspires.org

This organization sponsors the FIRST Robotics Competition, involving student-built robots competing against each other. The competition challenges participants to solve problems that involve science, technology, engineering, and math. FIRST LEGO League offers similar competitions for elementary and middle school students.

Software Engineer

What Does a Software Engineer Do?

Software engineers—also known as software developers—create, maintain, and improve computer software. They may work on any kind of software, from the games and applications that people use daily to the networks and operating systems that allow applications to run.

In the robotics industry, software engineering plays an essential role. "It is the medium to embody intelligence in the machine," writes the Robotics & Automation Society on their website. Components of a robot's intelligence may include programs that allow it to sense the world, process information, or take action.

Software engineers develop sets of rules, known as algorithms, that govern a robot's intelligence and behavior. One important component of this process is talking to customers to determine how they plan to use the robot. From this information, the software engineer will develop a list of requirements describing the functionality of the software he or she plans to develop.

At a Glance: Software Engineer

Minimum Educational Requirements
Bachelor's degree

Personal Qualities
Must enjoy problem solving, logic, and technology; close attention to detail; creative and can work well on a team

Certification and Licensing
Voluntary

Working Conditions
Indoors

Salary Range
About $56,310 to $149,480

Number of Jobs
As of 2014 1,114,000 in the United States

Future Job Outlook
A growth rate of 17 percent through 2024

The software engineer must decide whether to write new software or modify existing software. Then he or she will plan out the software systems and algorithms needed to make the robot behave as desired. This typically involves creating diagrams or flowcharts to model different aspects of the robot's behavior. Some software engineers write the computer code to implement their programs, but most rely on programmers to do this part of the work. The engineer remains involved in the process from beginning to end, however. He or she must keep accurate records of the development process, test the software to make sure it is working as desired, help fix "bugs" (technical issues that arise), and carefully document the software so that future developers can maintain or upgrade it as needed. Tim Perkins is a software engineer at Rethink Robotics in Boston, Massachusetts. On the company's blog, he said that his typical day includes "writing code, talking to teammates to coordinate work, designing new features based on customer feedback, learning new tech, fixing bugs, etc." He added, "Teamwork is key especially between the various groups."

How Do You Become a Software Engineer?

Education

Most software engineers have their bachelor's degree in computer science or a related engineering field. All computer science degree programs include classes in programming and mathematics. Students interested in software engineering for robotics should also choose courses on probability, artificial intelligence, computer vision, movement control, and sensor systems.

Some software engineers go on to get a master's degree or even a PhD. This level of education is typically only required for highly specialized positions in the robotics industry, such as in artificial intelligence or machine learning.

However, not all software engineers have a formal education in the field. Perkins studied electrical engineering and later transitioned to working on software. Practical experience coding and developing software systems or applications is extremely important. In addition, many employers test software engineers during the hiring process. The test may include programming tasks along with technical questions.

Sam Schillace is vice president of engineering at a technical company. In an article for *U.S. News & World Report*, he talked about how he decides whether to hire a software engineer:

> It's super important to understand CS fundamentals like big O notation, common algorithms, standard languages and technical approaches. You can learn this from school or from apprenticeship, but you need to learn it somehow. . . . We look at track records as much as school—someone from a great school with no outside coding projects or interesting technical accomplishments is definitely less interesting, and someone who is a rock star coder with no degree but a huge list of achievements would be an easy hire.

Even after they land a job, software engineers must continue to educate themselves to stay up-to-date on changes to programming languages, technologies, and other technical advancements.

Certification and Licensing

Certification is not usually required to work as a software engineer. However, certification is available for many different programming languages and software platforms. For example, a software engineer who works on applications for the Windows store may choose to become a Microsoft Certified Solutions Developer. This certification may make him or her more likely to be hired to work on projects for the Windows store.

Internships

Internships are plentiful for students studying computer science or software engineering. Top companies around the world are looking to hire software engineers, and an internship is a great way to get a foot in the door. A computer science intern may make anywhere from $15 to $30 an hour. Many internships lead to a job offer with the company.

Skills and Personality

Software engineers encounter difficult problems every day. Often, they face problems that no one has solved yet. Coming up with a solution requires highly technical skills as well as curiosity, creative thinking, keen intelligence, and the ability to stay focused for long periods of time. At the same time, software engineers must be able to clearly communicate their ideas to others, as they almost always collaborate on a team. Chuck Lloyd works on software systems at Rethink Robotics. On the company's blog, he described how a software engineer must be the kind of person who constantly seeks to improve his or her skills, even if that means making mistakes:

> A really good software programmer wants to be a better programmer. That means they are open to a constant process of trying new things. It also includes finding a way to learn from other programmers. If you can't keep an open mind and work with people, I think you will fall behind. . . . I've been writing software for a while. I've done some really brilliant things and some stupendously dumb things. You have to be able to laugh and learn from your mistakes and not get too caught up in your success.

Tom Janofsky, vice president of software engineering at a technology company in Philadelphia, agrees that dealing with failure is an important skill for software engineers. He explains why in an article in InformationWeek: "A lot of what we do is about failing, doing something wrong and then going back and looking at the problem again. Our work is a puzzle and that's a great part of the job that's often not seen or understood."

Employers

Nearly every industry in the world today relies on computers and computer programs. Software engineers are in high demand to develop these programs. As new technology platforms become more common, businesses will need software engineers to move their data, services, and products over to the new platform. For example, many software engineers today are developing applications for tablets and other mobile devices. In the future, cutting-edge technology such as virtual reality or robotics will likely become the focus of most new software development.

According to the Bureau of Labor Statistics (BLS), current software engineering jobs are spread throughout many different industries. Thirty-three percent work in computer systems design and related services. Eight percent work for software publishers, another 8 percent in finance and insurance, and 8 percent in computer and electronic product manufacturing. Robotics is a highly specialized field, and jobs in this particular area will likely be more difficult to find compared with other more common industries.

However, all robotics companies need software engineers. ABB Robotics, Aethon, Kawasaki Robotics, and Yamaha Robotics all build robots for industrial use. General Dynamics, ReconRobotics, Raytheon, and Lockheed Martin produce robots for the military. NASA develops robots to explore outer space and other planets. Technology giants such as Google, Microsoft, and Apple also hire software engineers for a variety of different projects, including some that involve robotics or artificial intelligence.

Working Conditions

Software engineers typically work indoors in an office environment. They spend a lot of time at a computer and may have the option to telecommute, or work remotely. However, most software engineers work closely in person with a small team of other programmers and engineers.

Most positions are full-time. When a project is nearing completion, software engineers often have to put in long hours. Fifty-hour weeks are common for some in this profession. For this reason the job can be stressful.

The field of software engineering is also looking to expand the diversity of employees. Over 90 percent of software engineers are men and over 90 percent are white or Asian. Technology companies would love to welcome more women and minorities into these roles.

Earnings

According to the BLS, software engineer salaries ranged from around $57,340 on the low end to upwards of $153,710 as of 2015. The median wage was $98,260. That is nearly three times higher than the median wage for all occupations in the United States. Software engineers working in the robotics industry can expect a similar salary. The cities of San Jose, San Francisco, and Santa Rosa in California, as well as Seattle, Washington, and Baltimore, Maryland, offer the highest salaries for software engineers.

Opportunities for Advancement

A software engineer will typically receive a promotion after three to five years on the job. From an entry-level position, he or she may move up to several different senior-level positions. A role that designs more advanced software is typically referred to as lead software engineer, software architect, or senior software engineer. As an alternative, a software engineer may take on more leadership responsibility in project management or team leadership.

What Is the Future Outlook for Software Engineers?

In 2016, *U.S. News & World Report* ranked software developer as the thirteenth best out of all possible jobs, and the second-best technology job. The job earned this ranking thanks to its high median salary, low unemployment, high rate of growth, and high number of positions available. The BLS predicts a 17 percent growth rate through 2024, which is more than twice the predicted growth rate for all occupations.

Most of the demand for software engineers will come from the health and medical industry and from companies producing applications for tablets, mobile devices, and other new technologies. Some of these exciting new technologies will likely be robots. Shiwei Wang, a software engineer at Rethink Robotics, is excited about her profession's future. On the company's blog, she said: "I feel very positive about robotics because it has so much potential. In the next few years robots will be doing new, exciting tasks. As a robot maker, I feel excited about how I'll be able to contribute and make my mark on the industry. I'm very excited to see what the future brings."

Association for Women in Computing (AWC)
PO Box 2768
Oakland, CA 94602
website: www.awc-hq.org

The AWC strives to help women advance in computing professions, including programmers and software engineers. The organization offers opportunities for professional growth through networking and programs on technical and career-oriented topics.

Association of Software Professionals (ASP)
PO Box 1522
Martinsville, IN 46151
website: www.asp-software.org

The ASP community brings software developers together to share their experiences creating and mastering different technologies and working through business challenges. Members of the ASP create desktop and laptop programs, software as a service applications, cloud computing, and mobile apps.

Object Management Group (OMG)
109 Highland Ave.
Needham, MA 02494
website: http://robotics.omg.org

The OMG is a group that promotes standards for programming languages and other technologies. The Robotics Domain Task Force applies these standards to robotics systems. The group also works to educate others about technology standards.

Robot Operating System (ROS)
website: www.ros.org

ROS is a great way to begin trying out software development for robotics. The organization's collections of free tools, libraries, and other information help software developers collaborate on robotics projects. In the ROS community, developers offer advice and support to each other.

FIRST
200 Bedford St.
Manchester, NH 03101
website: www.firstinspires.org

This organization sponsors the FIRST Robotics Competition, involving student-built robots competing against each other. The competition challenges participants to solve problems that involve science, technology, engineering, and math. FIRST LEGO League offers similar competitions for elementary and middle school students.

Computer Programmer

What Does a Computer Programmer Do?

> **At a Glance:**
> ### Computer Programmer
> **Minimum Educational Requirements**
> Associate's degree
>
> **Personal Qualities**
> Analytical; well disciplined; and able to maintain focus; creative; enjoy problem solving
>
> **Certification and Licensing**
> May be required for a specific programming language
>
> **Working Conditions**
> Indoors at a computer, sometimes solitary
>
> **Salary Range**
> About $44,450 to $130,800
>
> **Number of Jobs**
> As of 2014 328,600 in the United States
>
> **Future Job Outlook**
> Declining growth rate for generalists but rising demand for programmers specializing in robotics

A computer programmer writes and edits the code that makes computer software run. Typically, software developers and engineers design the software while programmers convert those plans into actual code. Programmers also spend a lot of time testing software. When they find bugs, or technical issues, they must go into the code to find and fix the problem.

Computer software can be written in a number of different programming languages, such as C# or Java, and can run on many different operating systems, or platforms, such as OSX or Android. Most programmers focus on one or two platforms, and work primarily in a couple of programming languages, but they may be familiar with many more. The general approaches to solving programming problems are the same no matter what language the programmer is working with. That said, programming languages and operating systems evolve and change over time. Programmers must stay up-to-date to keep their skills sharp.

Today, many devices besides computers run software programs. Mobile phones, tablets, and video game systems all run applications that someone had to program. Cars, home appliances, cash registers, and other machines also rely on computer programs. In the robotics industry, computer programmers work on software and applications to guide the behavior of various robots.

All of these programmers spend their days solving problems. In a video for the Alberta Learning Information Service, computer programmer Steven Dytiuk describes his job:

> A typical day for me starts at around 8 am. You have a list of tasks to do, and those will usually have a design already associated. Some tasks take just hours to do. Some tasks take weeks to do. [For] some things you work independently, and some things you work on a team. . . . You might be coding in C#, you might be doing web based applications, or you might be doing database programming . . . but the solution you're providing needs to have good performance and meet the needs of the client.

At a company that designs and builds robots, a team of engineers and computer programmers designs, builds, and tests the software that forms a robot's "brain." The robot will come with the ability to perform a set of basic tasks. However, most robots are customizable. For example, the customer may need to program the robot to grab an item of a certain shape, or to recognize defects on a part. Usually, the robot manufacturer has developed its own custom programming language to go with the robot.

A robot programmer is a specialized role that requires learning the custom language and providing instructions to prepare a robot to perform a specific task. A robot programmer often works for the company that designs the robot and travels to assist customers with installation or troubleshooting. Robot programmers or computer programmers may also need to assist customers as they integrate robotic solutions with existing software systems. For example, an existing product database may need to link with a new robotic warehouse.

The problems that programmers face in their daily work may never have been solved before. Dytiuk describes how he approaches solving such a problem: "You get the problem and you have to think about it and strategize and work together on a team, because one person usually can't figure it out on his own. Once you work hard and build that solution, then deliver it, it feels awesome."

How Do You Become a Computer Programmer?

Education

Most computer programmers get a four-year degree in computer science or a related field, but some jobs may require only an associate's degree or postsecondary certificate from a two-year program at a community college, vocational school, or technical school. In rare cases computer programmers may get hired without a formal education, as long as they have demonstrated strong programming skills. Misha Gorodnitzky is now a software engineer at Digital Science. But he started out in a technical support role. In a video interview for the website icould, he said: "I didn't finish high school because I was too busy writing computer programs at home. I'm completely self-taught from the very beginning." This type of story was much more common when computers were new technology and most high schools and colleges didn't yet offer courses that taught skills programmers needed.

Today, programming courses are much more widely available. In addition, it's easier than ever for people with an interest in programming to get started at home. All they need is a computer. No matter what level of education they achieve, it's essential for computer programmers to gain experience writing actual programs. Many employers expect to see a portfolio of completed work when considering candidates for a programming job. Employers also often test programmers during the hiring process with programming tasks and technical questions.

In the field of robotics, computer programmers write and edit the code that makes the software and applications that guide robot behavior. They also test software for bugs, and when they find them, go into the code to fix the problem.

A person interested in both programming and robotics should study areas of programming related to how robots move and make decisions, such as motion and path planning, decision processes, and search algorithms. Hands-on experience in robotics is also important, and one way to gain that experience is through robotics competitions. Though people tend to think of these as engineering competitions, computer programming is also essential to control the robots' actions. In the FIRST Robotics Competition, teams of high school students get six weeks to build a robot that will have to play a game against other teams' robots. The competition challenges participants to solve problems that involve science, technology, engineering, and math. FIRST LEGO League offers similar competitions for elementary and middle school students.

Certification and Licensing

Certification is fairly common among computer programmers and robot programmers. A company may require programmers to gain certification in a specific programming language, such as C++, or in tools related to their work. For example, Microsoft Certified Solutions Developer is a certification that proves expertise in programming for Microsoft products, including the Windows store and web applications.

Common certifications for programmers working in robotics include MATLAB—software that enables technical design—and programmable logic controllers (PLCs), a control system for industrial computers used in manufacturing.

Internships

Internships are a common way for programming students to gain experience. Typically, students complete internships while still in school. Students in bachelor's degree programs in computer science will have an easier time landing an internship than students in an associate's degree program. Employers are most interested in people who have invested that extra time and money into developing a standard set of programming skills.

Robot programming, however, is a very specific skill within manufacturing. Students in a two-year degree program to learn robot programming should not have trouble finding internships with manufacturers.

Skills and Personality

Like software engineers, computer programmers often face problems that no one has solved yet. Coming up with a solution requires technical skill, creative thinking, intelligence, and the ability to concentrate for long periods of time. Programmers must also be able to clearly communicate their ideas to others. Though some programmers spend a lot of time working from home or in a solitary environment, they will eventually have to present their work to a customer or team.

In the Alberta Learning Information Service video, David den

Otter, regional manager of a computer company, described what he looks for when hiring a computer programmer: "We're looking for someone who's smart, able to take complicated problems and think them through, break them down into bite-sized pieces. They have to like to be creative, to be challenged, they also have to be able to work in teams with others and really like a lot of variety in what they do."

Employers

Almost every industry in the world today needs programmers and software engineers. While the demand is much higher for software engineers with a four-year degree, many of these engineers get their start with a job or internship as a programmer. According to the Bureau of Labor Statistics (BLS), 38 percent of computer programming jobs are found in computer systems design and related services.

Robot programming is a specialized job in the manufacturing industry. Companies that hire robot programmers include ABB, a maker of industrial robots; A.O. Smith, a company that produces water technology; and KeyMe, a New York–based company that builds robotic kiosks to copy keys.

Working Conditions

Computer programmers work indoors at a computer. Many work in an office alongside other programmers and engineers. However, as programming work can be done from anywhere, many computer programmers telecommute. Dytiuk says, "Software programmers have a lot of flexibility in location. . . . I can work from home if I'd like to." He adds that the job can require putting in extra effort to meet deadlines. "In this industry deadlines are really important. You'll find that some evenings you end up having to work, or some weekends depending how things are going."

Robot programmers work in factories, typically on manufacturing floors. They may have to travel extensively to program robots for customers.

Earnings

Computer programmers typically earn between $44,450 and $130,800, according to the BLS. As of 2015 the median wage was $79,530. That is more than double the median wage for all occupations in the United States. Programmers at software publishers typically make more than those working in manufacturing or computer systems design.

Opportunities for Advancement

Computer programmer is a common first job for students who graduate with a bachelor's degree in computer science. After a few years of experience, most computer programmers will earn a promotion. Dytiuk describes the two directions a typical programming career takes: "You either start supervising people and you work towards management, or you can become really specialized in your area of technical expertise and become a specialized engineer or technician." Along the way, many programmers earn the title of software engineer or software developer.

In order to advance, a computer programmer must continuously update his or her knowledge of programming languages, operating systems, and other related tools. Technology changes rapidly, and a programmer has to work hard to keep his or her skills relevant to the current market.

What Is the Future Outlook for Computer Programmers?

The BLS predicts that employment of computer programmers will drop 8 percent through 2024. Yet the number of available jobs for software engineers in the United States should grow 17 percent over the same time period. The reason for this huge difference in job outlook is that programming is typically a solitary job that can be done remotely, so companies can outsource these jobs to workers overseas. In order to be competitive in the job market in the United States, a computer programmer should set his or her sights on gaining enough education and experience to advance to a software engineering role.

Meanwhile, job opportunities for robot programmers are plentiful. CNN named "robot programmer" one of the hottest new jobs of 2007—and the robotics industry has continued to grow since then. Manufacturing firms are having trouble finding enough programmers with expertise in robotics, and especially in PLCs, according to an article in *Fortune* magazine titled "Revenge of the Robotics Nerds: They're in Demand." In the article, engineering executive Andrew Valentine says: "I would hire at least 20 more full-time PLC programmers if I could find them."

Find Out More

Association of Software Professionals (ASP)
PO Box 1522
Martinsville, IN 46151
website: www.asp-software.org

The ASP community brings software developers together to share their experiences creating and mastering different technologies and working through business challenges. Members of the ASP create desktop and laptop programs, software as a service applications, cloud computing, and mobile apps.

National Association of Programmers (NAP)
PO Box 529
Prairieville, LA 70769
website: www.napusa.org

The NAP is a professional organization dedicated to programmers, developers, consultants and other professionals and students in the IT industry. It provides information and resources to guide those in this field and also offers a professional certification.

Object Management Group (OMG)
109 Highland Ave.
Needham, MA 02494
website: http://robotics.omg.org

The OMG is a group that promotes standards for programming languages and other technologies. The Robotics Domain Task Force applies these standards to robotics systems. The group also works to educate others about technology standards.

Robot Operating System (ROS)

website: www.ros.org

ROS is a great way to begin trying out software development for robotics. The organization's collections of free tools, libraries, and other information help software developers collaborate on robotics projects. In the ROS community, developers offer advice and support to each other.

FIRST

200 Bedford St.
Manchester, NH 03101
website: www.firstinspires.org

This organization sponsors the FIRST Robotics Competition, involving student-built robots competing against each other. The competition challenges participants to solve problems that involve science, technology, engineering, and math. FIRST LEGO League offers similar competitions for elementary and middle school students.

Robot Operator

What Does a Robot Operator Do?

A robot operator is the person who oversees or controls a robot as it works. While most robot operators work on factory assembly lines, other industries such as construction and energy production are also beginning to rely more heavily on robots. Some police officers and soldiers operate flying drones or robots that detect and defuse explosives. Some scientists even operate robots working in space or in the deep sea.

In the manufacturing industry, robot operators are known as computer-controlled machine operators or computer numerical control (CNC) machine operators. This is a specialized role within the broader category of machinists. Machinists are people who operate machines to produce parts or instruments, typically according to instructions from an engineer. Machinists set up machines according to documentation, monitor machines for unusual activity, insert material into machines, remove finished products, and test finished

At a Glance: Robot Operator

Minimum Educational Requirements
High school diploma or equivalent

Personal Qualities
An understanding of machinery; enjoyment of hands-on work; attention to detail; ability to work well under pressure

Certification and Licensing
Voluntary

Working Conditions
Typically in a factory or outdoors; safety equipment is often required

Salary Range
About $25,230 to $61,290*

Number of Jobs
As of 2014 about 477,500 in the United States*

Future Job Outlook
10 percent growth predicted between 2014 and 2024*

*Numbers are for machinists, a group that includes computer-controlled machine operators.

products to ensure that they meet specifications. Computer-controlled machine operators do not have to manually control the machine. Instead, they program it to perform its tasks, then oversee its work.

Computer-controlled machine operators tend to specialize in a specific kind of machine, such as a CNC lathe or mill. Both of these machines cut metal, plastic, or wood into a variety of customizable shapes. Robotic welders are also becoming more common. Welding is a process that uses high heat to join metal pieces together. A robot operator oversees the robotic welder's work to ensure that it is functioning properly and producing quality work.

Adam Firkus is a machinist who works with CNC lathes and mills. In a video by his company, Waupaca Foundry, he said:

> We start out with raw stock. There's a broad category of tooling that you get to choose from. There are so many different ways to complete a part. . . . We program each line, each circle that we're going to have the cutter cut . . . from there on the machine will run the path that you program for it. It feels really good that you created something.

Robot operators also work in industries other than manufacturing. In construction most machinery still requires a human driver. However, new automated cranes, excavators, bricklayers, wall assemblers, and more don't require a human to sit inside it at the controls. Yet an operator still needs to program each machine or drive it from a remote station. In the energy industry, robotic systems are used to perform repairs on buried gas pipelines. An operator helps run and maintain the system.

Robot operators even have a place in the military and police force. A soldier or police officer may specialize as an explosive ordnance disposal operator, working either at home or in an active war zone overseas. This technical specialist conducts operations to locate unexploded devices, or responds to incidents and emergencies involving explosive devices. Then he or she will control a robot to dispose of the threat. A soldier may also become an unmanned aircraft systems operator. These operators use remote control systems to direct drones—which are basically flying robots—to perform surveillance on remote locations.

Finally, a select few robot operators get to explore outer space or the deep sea. These operators are typically trained scientists with master's degrees or even PhDs. At NASA, Julie Townsend enters the instructions that tell the rover *Opportunity* where to drive on the surface of Mars. In an interview on NASA's website, she said:

> I've been involved in every phase of the mission, from development through launch, to landing and operating on Mars. Now, I hold the coveted position of Rover Planner, also called Rover Driver, and I'm responsible for creating the command sequences that move the rovers and their robotic arms around on the Martian surface.

How Do You Become a Robot Operator?

Education

Getting a job as a CNC machine operator in manufacturing or as a robot operator in construction or energy technology usually only requires a high school diploma, though some employers may look for an associate's degree from a technical school or community college. Candidates without a degree are more likely to get hired if they've taken high school courses in computer programming, math, and machine shop. Some employers will pay for CNC machine operators to complete a two-year vocational program while working. Almost all CNC machine operators receive on-the-job training as well. Some employers offer apprenticeship programs in which the new employee learns from a seasoned worker.

Explosive ordinance disposal jobs on the police force or in the military require special training. A person who is already a police officer needs about five years of experience on the job before being considered as a bomb tech. Then he or she would have to wait for an opening, try out for the job, and complete rigorous training if selected. A soldier interested in this career must take a series of tests called the Armed Services Vocational Aptitude Battery. These tests help determine what type of job is the best fit for the soldier. If selected for explosive ordinance disposal, the soldier would have to complete ten weeks of basic combat training and thirty-seven weeks of advanced individual training.

Finally, the scientists who direct robots to explore the deep sea or other planets typically have master's degrees or PhDs in an engineering field or computer science. They also are usually involved in scientific research projects related to the mission.

Despite the varied educational requirements, all jobs with robots require hands-on experience. Julie Townsend explains why that is so important:

> You can't really learn robotics from any textbook or homework assignment. The only way to demonstrate that you can make machines work is to build some machines and make them work! These days there are lots of opportunities for kids to build and compete: solar cars, model rockets, underwater robots, robots for competitions like BEST (BEST stands for "Boosting Engineering, Science, and Technology") or FIRST or VEX or others. Find an opportunity to design, build, program, and/or operate something!

Certification and Licensing

A growing number of employers prefer to hire CNC machine operators with certification. However, not all operators must obtain certification before getting a job. Some employers may even pay for an employee to complete a certification program. Professional organizations such as the National Institute for Metalworking Skills or the Manufacturing Institute offer certification in a variety of CNC machines and other related skills.

Internships

Many technical degree programs in manufacturing include a paid internship component. The internship provides hands-on experience in a work environment and often leads to a permanent job offer once the student has completed his or her degree.

Skills and Personality

All robot operators, whether employed in manufacturing or other fields, must have an affinity for machinery, computer skills, and excellent dexterity for hands-on work. They should not be afraid of getting their hands dirty—literally, as some positions require outdoor work at a construction site or even on the battlefield. Computer skills are also very important as almost all operators are responsible for programming robots or other machines as needed. In manufacturing, physical strength and stamina are also important as the operator may be on his or her feet working with heavy equipment all day. It takes a special personality to work as a bomb disposal technician or drone operator. These soldiers and police officers must work calmly under stress and must be willing to put themselves in danger in order to protect others.

On the Job

Employers

In manufacturing the biggest employers of CNC machine operators are machine shops, motor vehicle manufacturers, metal product manufacturers, and aerospace manufacturers. The motor vehicle and aerospace industries offer the best pay for these positions. While jobs are fairly evenly distributed across the United States, the highest concentration is in the Midwest.

The US government employs robot operators in the military and in various areas of scientific research. At NASA, robot operators program and control robots to explore outer space or other planets. Scientists at the National Oceanic and Atmospheric Administration operate robotic submarines for deep-sea exploration.

Working Conditions

Working conditions for robot operators vary greatly, depending on the industry. In manufacturing, CNC machine operators often work on factory floors. The environment may be noisy and full of machinery. As a safety precaution, these workers may be required to wear safety glasses, earplugs, steel-toed boots, or other protective clothing. In the plastics industry, respirators protect workers from fumes. CNC machine operators typically work full-time. Since most factories operate around the clock, these operators may need to work in the evenings, on the weekends, or at night.

Some positions require outdoor work—for example, at an excavation site near a gas pipeline. Soldiers or police officers who operate bomb disposal robots often work in stressful, dangerous situations—outdoors and indoors. They may be called upon at all hours of the day or night.

Earnings

CNC machine operators are usually paid hourly. According to the Bureau of Labor Statistics (BLS), the rate ranges from $11.73 per hour to $27.34. An hourly position gives the operator the opportunity for overtime pay if he or she works more than forty hours in a week. This hourly rate works out to an annual income between $24,210 and $56,860.

Robot operators in the military receive the same kinds of compensation as all military members. This includes housing, medical, food, special pay, and vacation time. They may also receive full scholarships to attend college or technical school.

Opportunities for Advancement

As they gain more and more experience on the job, CNC machine operators will receive higher pay and additional responsibilities. Those with excellent technical skills may move up into a new position in machinery maintenance, while those skilled in communication may become supervisors.

A robot operator advances through the ranks of the army or police force in the same manner as his or her colleagues. When certain conditions are met, such as time served or points earned, he or she will earn a more advanced rank, such as sergeant in the army or lieutenant on a police force.

What Is the Future Outlook for Robot Operators?

Robots and automated machines have gradually taken over many jobs that once belonged to people. The first jobs to go to robots are the ones that are boring or dangerous for human workers. Factory machinery used to require a lot of repetitive, manual operation. Bomb disposal was once an even riskier occupation than it is today. Now, workers can keep a safe distance and program robots to complete these tasks autonomously.

Stories about robots stealing human jobs abound in the media. However, new jobs with different skill sets are created to replace the ones that robots take over. Employers still need people to program and oversee the robots.

As a result, the job market for robot operators is growing. The BLS predicts 10 percent growth for machinists through 2024. This is slightly faster growth than average for all occupations. New types of robot operator jobs will be opening up all the time as new robots and computer-controlled machinery become available.

Find Out More

Fabricators & Manufacturers Association, International (FMA)
833 Featherstone Rd.
Rockford, IL 61107
website: www.fmanet.org

The FMA organizes educational programs, networking events, and trade shows for those involved with metal processing, forming, and fabricating, including machinists and CNC machine operators. A charitable foundation run by the organization provides grants to community and technical colleges to run manufacturing summer camps for students ages twelve to sixteen.

Manufacturing Institute
733 Tenth St. NW
Washington, DC 20001
website: www.themanufacturinginstitute.org

This organization works to develop manufacturing talent and attract the next generation of manufacturing workers, including robot operators. The Manufacturing Institute offers tool kits for employers, educators, and community leaders to implement certification programs.

NASA Career Corner
website: www.nasa.gov/audience/foreducators/robotics/careercorner/#.V5kDnJOAOko

NASA's career corner discusses how robot operators and other scientists working with the space agency's robots got started in their careers.

National Institute for Metalworking Skills (NIMS)
10565 Fairfax Blvd., Suite 10
Fairfax, VA 22030
website: www.nims-skills.org

The NIMS sets standards for the metalworking industry and offers certification programs for fifty-two distinct skills, including CNC milling and CNC turning, both important robot operator skills in the manufacturing industry. The association has also launched a program to help employers design and offer apprenticeships.

US Army
website: www.goarmy.com

To learn more about careers in the military that involve working with robots, look up information about becoming an explosive ordinance disposal specialist or an unmanned aircraft systems operator.

Sales Engineer

What Does a Sales Engineer Do?

A sales engineer sells technical products—such as software, computer processors, or robots—to businesses. In many ways the job is like any other sales position. The sales engineer must seek out new customers and interest them in the product. Then he or she must negotiate a price and seal the deal. He or she must also maintain relationships with existing customers. This includes responding to their issues or concerns and assisting them as needed.

When it comes to highly technical products such as robots, customers often have complex technical questions, or need help troubleshooting technical issues. For this reason, robotics companies often look to hire salespeople with backgrounds in engineering. The sales engineer must thoroughly understand how the robot works in order to address specific technical issues that customers face. The sales engineer must also be able to explain the robot in technical language for engineers and in simplified language for nontechnical customers.

At a Glance: Sales Engineer

Minimum Educational Requirements
Bachelor's degree

Personal Qualities
Strong interpersonal skills; self-confidence; charisma; a competitive spirit; keen technical ability

Certification and Licensing
Voluntary

Working Conditions
Indoors, travel required

Salary Range
About $55,280 to $165,250

Number of Jobs
As of 2014 69,900 in the United States

Future Job Outlook
Growth rate of 7 percent through 2024

At some companies, sales engineers work alongside sales representatives. In this case, the representative focuses on the sales side of the relationship with customers, while the engineer focuses on the technical side. One engineer may assist multiple salespeople with all of their customers. In this case, each salesperson would call on the engineer only when there is a technical issue that the salesperson can't handle alone.

The sales presentation is an important part of any job in sales. This is a meeting with a customer in which the salesperson explains the benefits of the product, how it fits the customer's needs, and why it's better than the competition. Before getting to a sales presentation, though, the salesperson must establish a relationship with potential customers through phone calls, e-mails, or visits. TEXMAC is a technology company based in Charlotte, North Carolina. In a job posting for a sales engineer in industrial automation, the company wrote: "This brand new opportunity is geared toward a hunter, someone who is not afraid to make the calls and face-to-face visits necessary to ask for and win business."

Winning new business and meeting quarterly sales goals is a huge part of any salesperson's job. The sales department is responsible for increasing a company's revenue and profits. However, sales engineers do much more. They often work closely with their customers' engineers to help solve problems. They may also customize their product to meet specific customer needs.

Texas Instruments is a company that produces computer chips and processors for electronic devices of all kinds, including robots. In a set of YouTube videos, technical sales representatives at the company explained why they enjoy their jobs. One sales rep, Kyle, said: "I don't really have a typical desk job. I'm pretty much on site with my customer every day, figuring out ways that TI can solve their challenges and improve their products. It's exciting being on the inside of working with the next big things." Another sales rep added: "I like solving problems. I get satisfaction from seeing a customer's product go from design all the way to production and helping their engineers every step of the way."

How Do You Become a Sales Engineer?

Education

Traditionally, almost all salespeople had bachelor's degrees or relevant work experience in business or marketing—even salespeople who worked at technology companies. But that has been changing. In fact, the job title "sales engineer" designates a salesperson with an engineering background. A bachelor's degree in an engineering, math, or computer science field is almost always required to become a sales engineer.

However, an engineering degree alone is not enough to prepare a person for this career. Michael Mullins is vice president of sales and marketing for a wireless software company in Reston, Virginia. He was quoted in an article on Monster.com: "They have to have that [charismatic] personality to make the leap. . . . There's a big difference between a successful salesperson and a successful engineer."

Because most engineering graduates did not take any courses in sales or business, many companies put engineers with the right personality for sales through special training programs. These programs typically teach best practices in sales and business as well as the technical particulars of that company's product. At the end of the program, the person will be ready to work as a sales engineer or technical sales representative.

Certification and Licensing

Most sales engineers do not need any certification or licensure. However, they may choose to get certified in a product or particular engineering field that is essential to their work. The National Council of Examiners for Engineering and Surveying develops and scores the exams needed to obtain a Professional Engineer license.

Darrin Mourer is a technical sales expert who edits the blog *The Sales Engineer*. In an article on the site, he wrote, "If you walk into an account right after [a sales engineer] from a different company pitching the same type of solution, who might a customer believe is more credible? Someone with no industry certifications or someone with 6 acronyms after their name?" He argues that getting certified could give a sales engineer that extra edge needed to land customers or a promotion.

Internships

Since most sales engineers earned a degree in a traditional engineering field, an internship or training program in sales is often essential to earning a permanent position in this field. "I've got a bachelor's and master's degree in electrical engineering," says Kyle of Texas Instruments. Yet before he became a technical sales representative, he went through three internships and a special training program. "It has been a great learning opportunity," he said.

Skills and Personality

The best sales engineers combine the technical expertise and problem-solving skill of an engineer with the drive, charisma, and persuasiveness of a salesperson. Someone who enjoys math, science, and tinkering with computers or machines, but also loves competition, traveling, and talking to people would do well as a sales engineer in any technical industry, from robotics to computer systems.

Zach is a sales manager at Oracle, a company that develops cloud applications and computer systems. In a video for the company, he described the kind of personality he looks for when hiring for his sales team: "I like athletes. I'm an athlete myself. I like people who are competitive. . . . I want people with the fire in their belly that want to be at Oracle." In the same video, another manager named Lionel added, "I'm looking for someone who's confident. Someone who has some thirst to learn. And someone who wants to make a difference."

On the Job

Employers

Most sales engineers work in technical fields. According to the Bureau of Labor Statistics (BLS), more than thirteen thousand people are employed in computer systems design. However, data processing and information services pay the highest wages to sales engineers.

Some sales engineers work for independent sales agencies. A sales engineer at an agency will work with several technical businesses to sell their products to customers.

The robotics industry also employs sales engineers. Industrial robotics companies such as ABB and Rethink Robotics hire sales engineers to work with manufacturers and factories that are interested in adding or upgrading robots on their assembly lines or in machine shops. These jobs may take the sales engineer overseas, as manufacturing is a huge industry in Asia.

Companies making robots for the medical industry, such as Corindus, also hire salespeople. However, instead of an engineering background, these technical salespeople must have medical experience or training.

Working Conditions

Travel is an important component of a sales engineer's job. The amount of travel required varies. Many sales engineers spend half of their time on the road. They may be away for days or weeks at a time visiting potential new clients, attending trade shows, or assisting current customers. While at home, sales engineers typically work in an office environment. While with customers, they often work in conference rooms or remote offices. Depending on the industry, their work may take them into a customer's factory or laboratory to work directly with their products.

Sales engineers may work irregular hours. They generally work full-time but often put in more than forty hours per week. Their travel schedules may also affect their hours. However, their schedules tend to be very flexible, and many sales engineers are able to telecommute, or work from home or the road, as needed.

Earnings

According to the BLS, sales engineers earn a salary between $55,280 and $165,250. As of 2015 the median income for this profession is $97,650. That's almost three times higher than the median income for all Americans.

However, salaries work a little differently for salespeople compared to other professions. Since sales feed directly into company revenue, most companies pay their salespeople a base salary plus commissions. Commissions are equal to a percentage of all sales that the salesperson makes. So, the better a salesperson performs, the better the company does, and the more money that salesperson will get to take home. Commissions are meant to motivate salespeople to make more sales.

Different companies offer a different balance of base pay and variable compensation. The variable compensation includes commissions and bonuses. A sales engineer may earn a bonus for job performance or for customer satisfaction. Typically, a sales engineer's salary will contain around 10 percent to 30 percent variable pay. This is lower than traditional sales roles, which are often entirely commission based. As a sales engineer gains experience and moves up in the ranks, the percentage of variable pay in his or her total salary will typically increase. Darrin Mourer explains: "The thought behind this is that as [a sales engineer] matures in grade, they are expected to pick up an increasing portion of the overall sale."

Sales engineers also usually get reimbursed for travel expenses, including airfare, lodging, and meals. Often, they'll even get reimbursed for entertaining customers with a dinner out, a sports game, or some other activity.

Opportunities for Advancement

Sales engineers may begin work right out of college, or they may get an entry-level job in engineering before moving into sales. There is a lot of room for upward movement in this role. A promotion for a sales engineer often comes with a higher commission rate, a larger sales territory, and a new job title, such as senior sales engineer or regional sales manager. From these roles, a successful sales engineer could eventually move up to become a national sales manager, vice president of sales, or business development director.

What Is the Future Outlook for Sales Engineers?

The BLS predicts a growth rate of 7 percent from 2014 through 2024 for sales engineers. This growth is the same as the average predicted for all occupations. Industries such as computer software and hardware and computer systems design, which could all include robotics systems, will likely see higher growth. Independent sales agencies will also likely grow in importance, as manufacturers outsource sales jobs.

Find Out More

Manufacturers & Agents (MANA)
6321 W. Dempster St., Suite 110
Morton Grove, IL 60053
website: www.manaonline.org

The MANA is a professional organization meant to foster good relationships between manufacturers and their representatives, including sales engineers who work for independent agencies in various industries, including robotics. The organization offers newsletters, webinars, seminars, and other educational opportunities.

Sales & Marketing Executives International (SMEI)
PO Box 1390
Sumas, WA 98295
website: www.smei.org

The SMEI is an organization that serves all sales and marketing professionals, including those working in robotics. Online forums, webinars, and other education opportunities allow members to connect and share knowledge. The SMEI also offers certification programs.

The Sales Engineer
website: www.thesalesengineer.com

This blog, edited by Darrin Mourer, includes a wealth of information on sales engineering, including tips on training, certification, sales presentations, career growth, and more. The information provided pertains to sales and engineering in any industry, including robotics.

FIRST
200 Bedford St.
Manchester, NH 03101
website: www.firstinspires.org

This organization sponsors the FIRST Robotics Competition, involving student-built robots competing against each other. The competition challenges participants to solve problems that involve science, technology, engineering, and math. FIRST LEGO League offers similar competitions for elementary and middle school students.

Product Designer

What Does a Product Designer Do?

A product designer, also known as an industrial designer, develops the look of a new product. People in this role are the inventors who imagine the objects people use in their day-to-day lives, from ceiling fans to cars. In the robotics industry, designers come up with the look and feel of a robot, from its features, body shape, and coloring to the user interface of its computer system. Product designers work closely with engineers, who are responsible for how the product works.

To develop the look of a product, the designer needs to figure out who will use the product and how it will be used. Usually, the designer meets with his or her team or a client to determine what is needed in the product design. The next step is to sketch out ideas, called renderings. These may be drawn on paper or in a computer program, such as computer-aided design (CAD). Product designers also build actual examples of the product, called prototypes, in a workshop or machine shop. They present their renderings and prototypes to the team. Throughout the whole process, the designer works closely with engineers and manufacturers to

At a Glance: Product Designer

Minimum Educational Requirements
Bachelor's degree

Personal Qualities
Creativity and artistic ability; mechanical, technical, and problem-solving skills

Working Conditions
Primarily indoors in an office setting

Salary Range
About $37,630 to $104,730

Number of Jobs
As of 2015 about 31,330 in the United States

Future Job Outlook
2 percent increase expected through 2024

make sure the product is safe, functional, and can be produced at a reasonable cost.

David Dymesich is the lead designer for Fetch Robotics, a start-up company creating robots for use in warehouses. He described his typical day in a video for the website the Muse:

> I'm design lead here at Fetch Robotics. My responsibilities are overseeing the entire design of the company—including the aesthetics of the robot, branding, all graphic design, user interface design. . . . I come in anywhere between 9 and 10. . . . I usually have to [inspect] some parts that come in, then settle into some design work. . . . I tend to call it a day around 7pm.

Some product designers do a lot of hands-on work building prototypes. Marek Michalowski cofounded the company BeatBots. His role in the company is to design cute, interactive robots used in childhood education. In a video by ConnectEd Studios, he said:

> I'm very often using my programming skills. I'm also using computer-aided design skills that I've taught myself over the last few years—and then, just knowledge of the tools in the machine shop, metalworking, woodworking, using a laser cutter, vinyl cutter, sewing machines. . . . But I would say the most rewarding thing is actually bringing these robots out into the world and seeing children's reactions.

How Do You Become a Product Designer?

Education

An entry-level job as a product designer typically requires a bachelor's degree in design or engineering. Many product designers attend art school, but industrial or product design degree programs can be found at technical universities and liberal arts colleges as well. These degree programs typically include courses in the principles of art and design, drafting, CAD, 3-D design, manufacturing methods, and engineering. Many product designers today go on to get a master's degree in design, engineering, or business as well.

For a product design job in robotics, an electrical, mechanical, or software engineering background is a necessary component. In fact, some robotics companies prefer to hire designers with engineering degrees rather than design degrees. In this case the job title may be design engineer rather than product designer.

In addition to developing technical skills, design students also keep a portfolio of their projects. This includes drawings and diagrams of product concepts, as well as any other visual material that demonstrates their design skill. A well-developed portfolio is key to getting a job as a product designer, and it may even be necessary to get into a degree program. For this reason, high school students interested in design should take art classes and keep a portfolio of their work. Seth Freytag is an industrial designer. In a video for the YouTube channel Major Decision, he described what his industrial design degree program was like: "I had to submit an exam and a portfolio of my work to be accepted into the program. . . . [The program] consisted of a series of studio classes . . . you have one product, one problem to solve. You create a solution where the form meets the function, and you've designed something."

Internships and Networking

Internships are a great way for a product designer to begin a career. Many design students complete summer internships while still in school. Students interested in designing robots should also participate in robotics competitions, such as FIRST. Although these competitions are geared toward engineers, they also help develop design and general problem-solving skills. In the FIRST Robotics Competition, teams of high school students get six weeks to build a robot that will have to play a game against other teams' robots.

Design can be a tricky field to break into. Finding a mentor can help a student gain the edge needed to embark on a career as a product designer. The mentor could be a teacher or working professional who is willing to take the time to introduce the student to others in the field, guide a job search, and answer questions about the career. Brian Ling is a designer at Design Sojourn, a design consultancy

Product designers who work in robotics come up with the look and feel of a robot, including its features, shape, and the user interface of its computer system. They work closely with engineers and others to test their ideas and to make sure the product is safe, functional, and not too costly.

firm. In a blog post on the company website, he talked about his experience with a mentor: "I have been blessed with someone that really took the time to look over my work and gave me fantastic feedback. I had met him when I interviewed for a job in his organization. He has somehow been quietly in the background all these years, giving me feedback or advice on and off."

Skills and Personality

A product designer must have a well-developed artistic eye along with technical aptitude. "The definition of design for me is a fusion between art and technology," said industrial designer Terence Woodgate in a panel discussion about design hosted by the company Heal's. Though Woodgate specializes in furniture and lighting design, his definition holds true for any kind of design, including robots. The art side of the equation involves creativity. Designers must be able to see possibilities for a product that others miss. They must come up with new, interesting, and original ideas on demand. However, they must also remain practical about their expectations.

In order to move forward, a product design idea must meet the customers' needs and fall within a reasonable price range.

When it comes to designing highly technical products such as robots, skill with machinery or knowledge of engineering is essential as well. The designer must understand how his or her design decisions will affect the way the robot functions.

Whether they're working on a robot that will educate kids or a kitchen faucet, a product designer also needs exceptional communication skills. Designers almost always work on teams. They must be able to give and receive criticism, explain their ideas thoroughly, and maintain happy relationships with their coworkers. Determination, enthusiasm, and the ability to work well under pressure are all important skills as well. Jordan Bahler is an industrial designer at Delta Faucet. In a video in the web series Artrageous with Nate, she explains why working together is so important: "It's essential to get collaboration with every one else. A lot of times I'll say this is so close, something's not right. I'll take it over to one of my colleagues, and say, 'What do you think about this? What am I missing?' With design, sometimes you need people around. You need a second opinion."

Employers

Many product designers work as consultants, often at a consultancy firm. A company that is ready to produce a new product or modify an existing one may not want to hire a full-time designer. Instead, the company may choose to work with a consultancy firm until the product design is complete. Some product design consultants work freelance. They provide the services of a design consultancy firm on their own. This is really only possible, however, after the designer has established a name for him- or herself in the field.

Other product designers work at companies such as automobile manufacturers or home furnishing manufacturers. These businesses put out new product designs on a regular basis, so there is always work for designers. Some product designers work at start-ups, or new companies that are just beginning to develop a product idea. Fetch Robotics is one example of a start-up in the robotics field.

Working Conditions

While many product designers spend a large amount of time at a computer or drawing board in a typical office setting, their work also takes them to other places. They may spend time in a laboratory building or testing product prototypes alongside engineers. They may visit homes or work sites to see a current version of the product in action. They may also visit the factory that manufactures the product.

Earnings

Product designers are among the best paid of all employees working in the art and design industry. They make about $37,630 to $104,730 per year, according to the Bureau of Labor Statistics (BLS). As of May 2015, the median annual wage for product designers in the United States was $67,130, about twice as much as the median wage for all occupations.

Opportunities for Advancement

Product design is a competitive career that can be difficult to break into. However, an excellent designer who stands out from the crowd has a lot of opportunity for advancement. In a design consultancy firm or design department at a large company, this person may move up to a supervisory role as chief designer, lead designer, or design department head. Some companies expect designers to get a master's degree in business or industrial design before a promotion will be offered.

Product designers who make a name for themselves may choose to work freelance independently or open a new design firm. In contrast, some designers move into teaching positions at art schools or universities.

What Is the Future Outlook for Product Designers?

Product design is a competitive industry, with slower-than-average growth expected in the near future. The BLS predicts just a 2 percent increase through 2024. Product design is closely linked to manufacturing, and employment in this industry is expected to decline in the

United States. Product designers will have the best chance for a job if they are experienced with both two- and three-dimensional CAD and computer-aided industrial design. Product designers who work on precision instruments and medical equipment should find increasing opportunities for employment. Robots could fall into both categories.

AIGA

233 Broadway, 17th Floor
New York, NY 10279
website: www.aiga.org

AIGA is the oldest and largest professional organization for design. It works to enhance the value and deepen the impact of design in every industry, including robotics. Members include fans of design, students, educators, design professionals, and business owners.

Industrial Designers Society of America (IDSA)

555 Grove St., Suite 200
Herndon, VA 20170
website: www.idsa.org

The IDSA is a professional organization for industrial designers, including those working in robotics. The nonprofit organizes national and regional conferences and publishes several newsletters as well as a magazine. It also sponsors design excellence awards, including awards for college students.

Product Development and Management Association (PDMA)

330 N. Wabash Ave., Suite 2000
Chicago, IL 60611
website: www.pdma.org

The PDMA is a professional organization that focuses on product development and management, including innovation in robotics. The PDMA runs an annual conference, virtual meetings and webcasts, and gives out an annual Outstanding Corporate Innovator Award.

FIRST

200 Bedford St.
Manchester, NH 03101
website: www.firstinspires.org

This organization sponsors the FIRST Robotics Competition, involving student-built robots competing against each other. The competition challenges participants to solve problems that involve science, technology, engineering, and math. FIRST LEGO League offers similar competitions for elementary and middle school students.

Research Scientist

What Does a Research Scientist Do?

Research scientists work at the cutting edge of science and technology. They design and carry out experiments intended to discover new scientific knowledge or test existing theories. They then analyze the data from these experiments and publish their results. Research scientists work in every area of the sciences, including life sciences such as biology, earth sciences such as geology, medical research, industrial science, materials science, and of course computer science and robotics. In the field of robotics, they may work on developing or testing new robotics materials, technology, or computer systems.

> ### At a Glance:
> ### Research Scientist
>
> **Minimum Educational Requirements**
> Master's or doctorate degree
>
> **Personal Qualities**
> An inquisitive mind; excellent problem-solving skills; persistence, patience, and determination
>
> **Working Conditions**
> Typically indoors at a computer or in a laboratory
>
> **Salary Range**
> About $64,300 to $170,610
>
> **Number of Jobs**
> As of 2014 about 25,600 in the US*
>
> **Future Job Outlook**
> 11 percent growth predicted through 2024*
>
> *Numbers are for computer and information research scientists, a group that includes robotics researchers.

Research scientists almost always work with a team of other scientists, laboratory assistants, and graduate students. They carry out experiments following the scientific method. The team must keep careful and accurate records. In order to be accepted by the scientific community, the results of an experiment must be reproducible. Often, an experiment yields a large amount of data. The scientists must then sort through and analyze this information to figure out what it means.

Finally, a research scientist must share his or her findings with the scientific community. Most often, the team writes up the experiment as an article that is published in a scientific journal. Other times, they will present their work at a conference or meeting.

A research scientist's work often leads to new products or new technology. Chris Jones, the director for research advancement at iRobot, explained how this might happen in an interview on Kids Ahead.com:

> I manage a group of scientists and engineers who are tasked with defining and executing research projects that push the state-of-the-art in robotics. . . . Our team brainstorms new ideas and we work with academic partners and researchers to find interesting and novel directions to push robotics. . . . We had a sponsor come to us who was looking to build soft robots. This sponsor was interested to see if it was at all possible to build a robot that was completely soft and squishy. It had never really been done before, so we were looking at a variety of different approaches.

How Do You Become a Research Scientist?

Education

A research scientist must invest a lot of time and money into education. Most working research scientists have a doctorate degree, also known as a PhD. This is the highest academic designation possible. PhD students spend four to eight years completing the program, and this is after four or five years as an undergraduate student, plus two to three years in a master's program. In total a research scientist could spend ten to fifteen years or even more in college.

However, there are many opportunities for students interested in research science to get hands-on experience long before earning a PhD. While in high school, programs such as FIRST Robotics, Destination Imagination, and Odyssey of the Mind challenge kids to solve problems creatively. These programs develop math, science, and technology skills.

During undergraduate or graduate studies, students can find work as laboratory assistants for professors who are also scientists. Graduate students may contribute enough to an experiment to have their names listed on a published scientific paper. By the time a student enters a PhD program, he or she must be ready to carry out original experiments. In remarks on the website of Elsevier (a provider of scientific, technical, and medical information products), Andy Greenspon, a PhD student in applied physics at Harvard, explained the goal of a PhD program: "The goal is not to complete an assigned set of courses as in an undergraduate program, but to develop significant and original research in your area of expertise."

Greenspon suggests that taking some time off to get real-world work experience in a research laboratory is a good idea for students interested in possibly beginning a PhD program.

> I will be forever grateful that I chose to do research in a non-academic environment for a year between my undergraduate and PhD programs. It gave me the chance to get a feel for doing nothing but research for a full year. . . . While my boss determined the overall experimental design, I was able to make my own suggestions for experiments and use my own discretion in how to perform them. I presented this research at two national conferences as well—a first for me. I was also able to learn about other research being performed there, determine which projects excited me the most, and thus narrow down my criteria for a PhD program.

Volunteer Work, Internships, and Mentors

Some undergraduate students may be able to find paid laboratory assistant positions, but many labs recruit volunteers. Working or volunteering in a research scientist's lab is a kind of apprenticeship for students who hope to be research scientists themselves one day. Students may seek out volunteer work opportunities at the college they are currently attending, or even at a nearby school. Dave G. Mumby

Research scientists design and carry out experiments intended to discover new scientific knowledge or test existing theories. In the field of robotics, they may work on developing or testing new robotics materials, technology, or computer systems.

is a psychology professor at Concordia University in Montreal, Canada. In a blog post, he explained how to go about finding a volunteer research position: "There are a lot of volunteer opportunities, but one must go about finding them in the proper way . . . you need to ask individual professors about working in their labs. Send your email directly to a professor, stating your interests in volunteering some of your time to help out with his or her research. . . . You must target your requests, and you must be sincere."

Internships at companies or institutions that perform scientific research are another great way for undergraduate or graduate students to obtain research experience. NASA offers a Robotics Academy program. This ten-week internship assigns participants to a research project with NASA, a local industry, or an academic institution.

Mentors are also an unofficial but important part of the journey to becoming a research scientist. A mentor could be a professor, boss, acquaintance, or other experienced research scientist willing to take the time to offer advice and encouragement. Lonnie Love is a robotics researcher and engineer at Oak Ridge National Laboratory. In an interview on Energy.gov, he talked about how he had volunteered with the FIRST Robotics team at a local high school and then started mentoring three of those students. "I really believe kids interested in engineering and science need to be building things," he said. "Education is much more than class work. Also try to find a mentor, someone to give you meaningful and honest advice. I've been blessed by having some of the best."

Skills and Personality

First and foremost, a research scientist must be passionate about his or her chosen area of focus. Scientific research also requires attention to detail, analytical skills, logical thinking, and communication skills. Ingenuity and dedication are important in order to come up with new ideas for research, and to deal with research that doesn't turn out as expected. Lenore Rasmussen is a chemist who develops materials for use in robotics. In an interview with the author, she described what she looks for in a new hire at her laboratory: "Able to think outside of the box and not get frustrated because in a lot of our experiments some things work and some things don't work. But you learn as much from what doesn't work as what does work. So a sense of perseverance and resolve [is really important]."

Employers

Some research scientists work as professors at colleges and universities. These scientists obtain grant money or funding to finance their research work. They often hire undergraduate or graduate students to work on projects either as paid employees or volunteers. Once a student has received a PhD, he or she may seek work as a professor and academic researcher. However, these positions can be difficult to obtain and keep.

Outside of the academic world, many private companies perform scientific research. Research is especially huge in the medical industry, where scientists develop new drugs, medical procedures, or even medical robotics. Technology companies are also investing in research into robotics and artificial intelligence. Employers include giants such as Google, Apple, and IBM.

The US government also hires research scientists. In fact, almost a third of all computer and information research scientists work for the government, mainly in the Department of Defense, according to the Bureau of Labor Statistics (BLS). One branch of this department, the Defense Advanced Research Projects Agency (DARPA), funds a lot of robotics research. From 2012 to 2015, the DARPA Robotics Challenge offered prizes for robots that could complete a series of tasks that might be required of a search-and-rescue robot. NASA also sponsors research in robotics. On NASA's website, research scientist Joel S. Levine says, "I am working on the development of a robotic, rocket-powered airplane, ARES, to fly through the atmosphere of Mars about a mile above the surface and search for evidence of life on Mars."

Working Conditions

Research scientists usually work indoors in a laboratory setting. While a portion of their time is spent actively setting up, running, and monitoring experiments, they also typically spend a large amount of time on a computer analyzing data or performing administrative duties. Researchers employed by colleges and universities also give lectures or lead student research.

Ashitey Trebi-Ollennu is a research scientist and engineer at the NASA Jet Propulsion Laboratory. In an interview for NASA's website, he said: "I do have an office but I actually spend most of my time in the robotics lab or flight testbed or in the field either developing new robotics technologies or testing technologies."

Earnings

Research scientists can earn a high salary, often into the six figures. According to the BLS, computer and information research scientists (including those who work with robotics) earn around $64,300 to $170,610. Researchers employed by colleges and universities tend to hold temporary positions that don't pay as well compared to those who work for the government or in the industry. In addition, these scientists often have to seek out grant money or funding to finance their own work. Some of the highest salaries go to researchers working for private companies in computer science, information technology, and engineering.

Opportunities for Advancement

A research scientist working in industry may earn a promotion after about five years on the job into a role as a senior research scientist or staff scientist. From there, he or she may go on to become principal scientist, project manager, research and development manager, or director of research and development. These advanced roles offer higher salaries and additional managerial responsibilities.

In the academic world, research scientists compete for tenure. Tenure is the name for a permanent position, often with a guaranteed salary. Professors without tenure typically hold temporary positions, and may have to switch institutions often. However, the academic world gives researchers more freedom and ownership for their work. An academic research scientist may start his or her own company to sell technology that was developed in the lab.

What Is the Future Outlook for Research Scientists?

Job prospects are excellent for research scientists, especially for those with advanced degrees in computer science. According to the BLS, employment of computer and information research scientists will grow about 11 percent through 2024. That is faster than the average growth predicted for all occupations. Many companies are looking to hire people with a PhD in the sciences. As these highly skilled workers are rare, someone who has invested the time and effort to gain such an advanced education will almost certainly find a good job.

Find Out More

American Association for the Advancement of Science (AAAS)
1200 New York Ave. NW
Washington, DC 20005
website: www.aaas.org

The AAAS is a nonprofit organization dedicated to advancing science, engineering, and innovation throughout the world for all people. The group works to increase public engagement with science and technology through education and outreach. They run conferences, volunteer programs, and workshops. They also develop materials for science teachers and students.

Association for Women in Science (AWIS)
1667 K St. NW, Suite 800
Washington, DC 20006
website: www.awis.org

The AWIS brings together women working in science, technology, engineering, and mathematics, often abbreviated as STEM. Women are traditionally underrepresented in these fields, and the AWIS strives for equality and full participation of women in the sciences.

Institute of Electrical and Electronics Engineers (IEEE)
445 Hoes Ln.
Piscataway Township, NJ 08854
website: www.ieee.org

The IEEE seeks to advance technology for the benefit of humanity. As a trusted voice for engineering, computing, and technology information, the IEEE runs conferences, puts out publications, sets technology standards, and develops educational activities.

FIRST
200 Bedford St.
Manchester, NH 03101
website: www.firstinspires.org

This organization sponsors the FIRST Robotics Competition, involving student-built robots competing against each other. The competition challenges participants to solve problems that involve science, technology, engineering, and math. FIRST LEGO League offers similar competitions for elementary and middle school students.

Interview with a Robotics Engineer

Ty Tremblay received his master of science in robotics engineering from Worcester Polytechnic Institute (WPI) in 2013. He now works at Symbotic, a company that provides robotics solutions for warehouses and distribution centers. He spoke with the author about his career.

Q: Why did you become a robotics engineer?

A: I was going to be a chef. I was taking classes at the regional vocational school and high school. Then, I was running late one day and took a shortcut through a place where a high school FIRST Robotics team was practicing. They lost control of their robot. It ran me over, and pinned me up against the wall. That introduced me to robotics. I did FIRST for four years and never went to another culinary class. Then I found out about WPI. It's been robots all the way ever since.

Q: Can you describe your typical workday?

A: My company builds robotic warehouses. There will be two to three hundred robots driving around to pick up cartons to be built into pallets, which are then delivered to a grocery store or distribution center. I started out as a manufacturing test engineer working at headquarters to build and test robots. Now, I'm a field systems engineer. I go to sites where they're building multimillion dollar systems. The systems are composed of robots—hundreds of them driving around inside a warehouse. I run tests designed to make sure everything is working properly, and fix it if I need to. As a robotics engineer, I was uniquely suited to doing the mechanical engineering for the fixtures, the electrical engineering for the motors and sensors, and the software engineering to gather the data and generate the reports.

Q: Could you give an example of a problem you solved?

A: Our robots drive around inside a warehouse and communicate via a wireless network. One of our warehouses was having a problem where a lot of bots were disconnecting as they drove around the warehouse. Sometimes the bots would disconnect and then reconnect, sometimes the bots would stay disconnected and we'd have to send a human into the system to retrieve the bot. This was affecting warehouse throughput, and we like to minimize humans entering the system from a safety standpoint, so I was sent to the location to see what I could do.

After gathering data, I noticed that the disconnect events weren't related to any certain location inside the warehouse and that certain bots disconnected more than others. This led me to believe that it wasn't a network issue and was likely related to the bots themselves. After further investigation, I discovered that the antennas on the bots were not designed for high vibration environments and were getting damaged internally as bots drove around. We found a new antenna that was more resistant to vibration and replaced all of the bad antennas. Problem solved.

Q: What do you like most and least about your job?

A: I like most that I have a direct impact on what our company delivers. I can go out in the field and make a marked improvement. In terms of robotics engineering, my favorite part is I can speak the language of any engineer in the company, which I think is really powerful. If you can walk up to the mechanical engineers and discuss why they chose this certain bolt and then in the same day go to the software engineer and talk about messaging architecture—it makes solving problems within the company easier for me. What I like least would have to be that I'm traveling a lot. I spend 3 weeks at each site, and then one week working remotely from home. I've traveled to California, Virginia, New Jersey, Pennsylvania, New York, and Florida.

Q: What personal qualities do you find most valuable for this type of work?

A: In my job, good communication skills. When something is going wrong, I have to find a way to explain so they understand what's happening and what we're doing to work around it. Also problem solving. Robotics is such an interdisciplinary field. You can solve a problem in so many different ways, so you have to be able to think about mechanical, software, electrical, and whole system solutions, as well as how hard it will be and how much will it cost.

Q: How is robotics engineering different from other engineering fields?

A: One of the concerns for a lot of us going through the robotics engineering degree was the phrase, "jack of all trades and master of none." But a robotics engineer can build an entire product. You can write apps for phones, or web apps. You can do electrical engineering, including automation for your house. Mechanical engineering classes teach you how things work and how to fix things. My education in robotics engineering made me the best all around engineer that I could be. One of my best friends started out in robotics engineering, and double majored in that and computer science. Now he writes code for satellites.

Q: What advice do you have for students who might be interested in this career?

A: If you're into engineering in any way shape or form, FIRST Robotics is one of the best things that you can do when you're in high school. It's a program meant to inspire kids to see how cool science, technology, engineering, and math can be. The number one reason that I am successful today is this hands on experience.

In terms of actual classes, I would say physics is a very good background to start with. If your school offers any software classes, like C programming, it's good one to get a leg up on that. If you can come into college with an understanding of what code is, that's a huge advantage.

Other Jobs in Robotics

Accountant
Computer Hardware Engineer
Computer Numerical Control (CNC) Machine Operator
Customer Service Representative
Data Scientist
Design Engineer
Electrical Engineer
Electronics Engineering Technician
Explosive Ordnance Disposal Specialist
Field Applications Engineer
Human Resources Representative
Industrial Automation Engineer
Information Technology Specialist
Integrated Circuit Designer
Machinist
Marketing Specialist
Mechanical Engineer
Mechanical Engineering Technician
Procurement Manager
Project Manager
Public Relations Specialist
Quality Assurance Specialist
Quality Engineer
Robotics Installer
Robotics Trainer
Robot Programmer
Sales Representative
Systems Engineer
Test Engineer
Unmanned Aircraft Systems Operator

Editor's Note: The US Department of Labor's Bureau of Labor Statistics provides information about hundreds of occupations. The agency's *Occupational Outlook Handbook* describes what these jobs entail, the work environment, education and skill requirements, pay, future outlook, and more. The *Occupational Outlook Handbook* may be accessed online at www.bls.gov/ooh.

Index

Note: Boldface page numbers indicate illustrations.

Picture Credits

Cover: Depositphotos/ndoeljindoel

6: Steve Zmina

17: Shutterstock.com/bibiphoto

35: iStockphoto/vgajic

59: iStockphoto/boggy22

66: iStockphoto/luchschen

About the Author

Kathryn Hulick lives in Massachusetts with her husband and son, Seth. They like to hike, read, cook, visit the ocean, and play with their dog, Maya. Hulick has written many books and articles for children, about everything from outer space to video games.